We're Not Out
of the Woods Yet

Doonesbury books by G. B. Trudeau

Still a Few Bugs in the System
The President Is a Lot Smarter Than You Think
But This War Had Such Promise
Call Me When You Find America
Guilty, Guilty, Guilty!
"What Do We Have for the Witnesses, Johnnie?"
Dare To Be Great, Ms. Caucus
Wouldn't a Gremlin Have Been More Sensible?
"Speaking of Inalienable Rights, Amy . . ."
You're Never Too Old for Nuts and Berries
An Especially Tricky People
As the Kid Goes For Broke
Stalking the Perfect Tan
"Any Grooming Hints for Your Fans, Rollie?"
But the Pension Fund Was Just Sitting There
We're Not Out of the Woods Yet

In Large Format

The Doonesbury Chronicles
Doonesbury's Greatest Hits

a Doonesbury book by

G.B. Trudeau

We're Not Out of the Woods Yet

Holt, Rinehart and Winston
New York

Published by Holt, Rinehart and Winston,
383 Madison Avenue,
New York, New York 10017.

Published simultaneously in Canada by Holt, Rinehart and
Winston of Canada, Limited.

Library of Congress Catalog Card Number: 79-1919

ISBN: 0-03-049181-9

First Edition

Printed in the United States of America

The cartoons in this book have appeared in newspapers
in the United States and abroad under the auspices of
Universal Press Syndicate.

2 4 6 8 10 9 7 5 3 1

MAY I HAVE YOUR ATTENTION, PLEASE? STUDIO 54 REGRETS ANY INCONVENIENCE OUR PRIVATE PARTY HAS CAUSED THOSE OF YOU WHO DROVE ALL THE WAY INTO THE CITY.

TO MAKE UP FOR IT, LIZA MINELLI AND BIANCA JAGGER HAVE AGREED TO COME OUT AND SIGN AUTOGRAPHS FOR A WHILE.

WE DON'T WANT **AUTOGRAPHS!** WE WANT TO **GET IN!**

TAKE IT OR LEAVE IT.

IF THEY THROW IN HALSTON, I, FOR ONE, WILL GO QUIETLY.

GBTrudeau

MR. DUKE, YOU UNDERSTAND, OF COURSE, THAT AFTER THE BOURNE INCIDENT, THE PRESIDENT IS ANXIOUS TO FIND A REPLACEMENT WITH IN-CONTESTABLE REPUTABILITY..

REPUTABILITY? MR. POWELL, WHEN IT COMES TO DISTINCTION IN THE FIELD OF DRUG ABUSE, I HAVE WHAT YOU MIGHT CALL AN EMBARRASS-MENT OF RICHES!

WHY, LEADING AUTHORITIES THE WORLD OVER CAN'T SAY ENOUGH ABOUT MY WORK! HERE, LET ME PUT ON MY COLLEAGUE, DR. P. Z. RILEY, DISTINGUISHED PRO-FESSOR EMERITUS OF ALKA-LOID DERIVATIVES..

WHO?

NOW, FOR GOD'S SAKE, DON'T LET YOUR VOICE CRACK, BOY!

GBTrudeau

YES, THIS IS MRS. DAVENPORT.

MA'AM, I'M CALLING FROM ACCOUNTING WITH THE INFORMATION YOU REQUESTED..

YOUR HUNCH ABOUT THAT YOUNG LAWYER WAS RIGHT. HIS SALARY WAS INCORRECTLY PROGRAMMED IN THE COMPUTER. WE'VE READJUSTED IT DOWN TO HIS PROPER SCALE. I HOPE HE WON'T BE TOO INCONVENIENCED..

NO, NO, I'M SURE NOT. YOU CAUGHT IT EARLY. THANKS VERY MUCH..

GBTrudeau

OF COURSE, **ANY** KIND OF CONDO IS A TERRIFIC INVESTMENT THESE DAYS!

I'M SURE YOU MADE THE RIGHT DECISION, WOODY.

FOLKS, WE WANT TO THANK YOU ALL FOR COMIN' TO GRACELAND, AND WE APOLOGIZE FOR THE LONG WAIT..

THERE'S BEEN SOME CONGESTION AT ELVIS' GRAVE TODAY, BUT WE 'SPECT IT SHOULD BE THINNIN' OUT PRETTY SOON NOW..

EXCUSE ME, BUT COULD YOU TELL US HOW LONG THAT MIGHT BE? I'VE BEEN WAITING SINCE 5:30 THIS MORNING.

HOW MANY MOURNERS IN YOUR PARTY, HONEY?

JUST ONE. NONSMOKING.

GBTrudeau

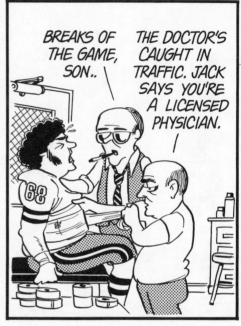

MY POINT, SIR, IS THAT WITH THREE PEOPLE HOSPITALIZED IN ONE GAME, SOMETHING HAS TO BE DONE!

LOOK, KID, I SYMPATHIZE, BUT WHAT CAN I DO? I'M ONLY ONE GENERAL MANAGER!

WHY, YOU COULD STAND UP TO THEM, SIR! YOU COULD PUBLICLY COME OUT IN FAVOR OF URINE TESTS!

URINE TESTS? OH, C'MON, RILEY, YOU KNOW HOW DEGRADING THAT IS TO THE PLAYERS?

OLYMPIC ATHLETES SEEM TO MANAGE, SIR.

THAT'S BECAUSE THEY'RE AMATEURS, BOY! THERE'S A BIG DIFFERENCE! AMATEURS AREN'T MATURE ENOUGH TO USE DRUGS!

IS THAT THE BEST YOU CAN DO, SIR?

LOOK, KID, MATURITY COUNTS! WHY DO YOU THINK THE NFL ONLY DRAFTS COLLEGE GRADUATES?

GBTrudeau

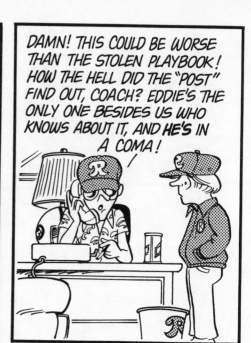

IT'S ALL THERE, DUKE—THE DRUGS, THE INJURIES, EVERYTHING! MY PHONE HASN'T STOPPED RINGING SINCE THE EARLY EDITION HIT THE STREETS!

DAMN! THIS COULD BE WORSE THAN THE STOLEN PLAYBOOK! HOW THE HELL DID THE "POST" FIND OUT, COACH? EDDIE'S THE ONLY ONE BESIDES US WHO KNOWS ABOUT IT, AND HE'S IN A COMA!

I DON'T KNOW, DUKE, BUT IF YOU DON'T TRACK THE LITTLE SNITCH DOWN FAST, YOU MIGHT AS WELL START PACKING!

TROUBLE, SIR?

IT JUST CAME TO ME, COACH.

IT WASN'T MY FAULT, SIR. THEY PLIED ME WITH CHEESEBURGERS.

GBTrudeau

..AND DESPITE MY HEATED PRO-TESTATIONS, EDDIE HAS CRAWLED FROM HIS HOSPITAL BED TO JOIN ME IN OUTRAGED DENIAL OF THIS ALLEGED PIECE OF REPORTING!

THIS ARTICLE REPRESENTS THE SHODDIEST KIND OF JOURNALISM! NAMES, DATES, PLACES ARE **ALL** INACCURATE! EVEN DOSAGES ARE DISTORTED AND TAKEN TOTALLY OUT OF CONTEXT!

AS EDDIE VIGOROUSLY CONFIRMS, THE "CONTROLLED SUBSTANCES" I GAVE HIM IN LAST SUNDAY'S GAME WERE NOTHING MORE THAN COMMON ASPIRIN TABLETS! RIGHT, EDDIE?

MMPHH.

NOW, I HOPE WE'VE HEARD THE LAST OF THIS SILLY EPISODE!

GBTrudeau

DAY TEN. THE MARCH TOWARD PEACE FLOUNDERS. AS TEMPERS FLARE AND ANTES ARE UPPED, JIMMY CARTER ACTS. A TOP AMERICAN NEGOTIATOR REMEMBERS.

WELL, HE SCHEDULED A MOVIE, "PATTON." IT WAS A RATHER COURAGEOUS ACT OF PROGRAMING, SINCE THE SAME FILM ONCE INSPIRED NIXON TO INVADE CAMBODIA.

THE EFFECT WAS QUITE DIFFERENT ON THE ISRAELIS, THOUGH. AFTER ONE ESPECIALLY GORY SCENE, DEFENSE MINISTER WEIZMAN ROSE AND CRIED OUT, "NEVER AGAIN!" THE IMPASSE WAS BROKEN.

COMING UP: PEACE ON THE RAMPAGE.

DAY 15: CAMP DAVID PLUS TWO. THE HISTORIC PEACE ACCORDS KINDLE AN OUTPOURING OF PUBLIC ACCLAIM!

FOR CARTER, SUCCESS IS SWEET. HIS STANDING WITH CONGRESS AND WITH THE AMERICAN PEOPLE HAS NEVER BEEN ON FIRMER GROUND.

CASE IN POINT: IN THE WAKE OF CAMP DAVID, A NEW POLL REVEALS THAT 93% OF THE PUBLIC NOW FEELS THAT PRESIDENT CARTER IS DOING AN EXCELLENT JOB FIGHTING INFLATION.

MOREOVER, 86% NOW APPROVE OF HIS HANDLING OF THE LANCE AFFAIR..

WELL, I ALWAYS HAVE.

ME, TOO. HE'S BEEN JUST GREAT!

DAY 16. BEFORE MR. BEGIN DEPARTS FOR HOME, HE GRANTS AN EXCLUSIVE INTERVIEW TO ABC NEWS. HE IS ASKED IF HE HAS ANY PLANS FOR TAKING A VACATION..

ABSOLUTELY NOT! AS I TOLD NBC YESTERDAY, THE STRUGGLE FOR US NEVER ENDS. THE JEWISH PEOPLE MUST NEVER LET DOWN THEIR GUARD AGAINST THE ENEMY!

WE HAVE SUFFERED FOR TOO LONG, WE HAVE ENDURED PERSECUTION, HORRIBLE WARS, AND THE THREAT OF EXTINCTION FOR OVER TWO THOUSAND YEARS, BEGINNING WITH..

ABC NEWS WITHDREW THE QUESTION. BACK AFTER THIS..

WHAT DO THE NEW ACCORDS SPELL FOR MR. BEGIN'S CAREER? IN A FAR-RANGING INTERVIEW, I ASKED THE DOUR LITTLE EX-TERRORIST ABOUT HIS POLITICAL FUTURE..

WELL, AS I TOLD CBS EARLIER, MR. HEDLEY, SOME FRIENDS WILL CRITICIZE ME. BUT THAT IS THEIR RIGHT. IT IS TO BE EXPECTED. THERE IS A PHILOSOPHICAL EXPRESSION FOR THIS..

SWITCHING FROM ENGLISH, MR. BEGIN THEN SPOKE DIRECTLY TO HIS OWN PEOPLE..

.."C'EST LA VIE."

CABIN FEVER PLUS TWO WEEKS. THE DRAMA COMES TO A CLOSE..

THE TWO WEEKS OF DAY-AND-NIGHT SUMMITRY FINALLY CATCH UP WITH AN EXHAUSTED PRESIDENT..

TAKING THE EVENING OFF, MR. CARTER HEADS OUT TO RFK STADIUM, WHERE HE IS THE HONORED GUEST OF THE MANAGEMENT OF THE WASHINGTON REDSKINS FOOTBALL CLUB..

JUST COFFEE. WHY?

FOR THIRTEEN STRAIGHT **DAYS**? C'MON, SIR, YOU CAN TELL ME!

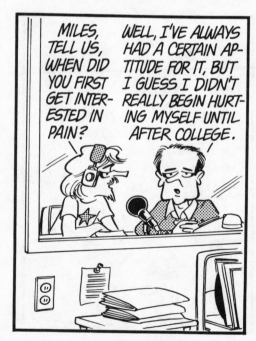

WELL! THE STUDENTS CERTAINLY SEEM TO BE FASCINATED BY YOUR MR. DUKE!

UH-HUH. SAY, WHO'S THE YOUNG LADY WHO HAS BEEN MONOPOLIZING HIM?

THAT'S MS. HUAN. SHE'S FROM PEKING.

ACCORDING TO HER, SHE AND MR. DUKE WERE CLOSE FRIENDS DURING HIS TOUR OF DUTY IN CHINA..

WILL YOU BE SHOWING ME WASHINGTON BY NIGHT, SIR?

CAN'T MAKE ANY SUDDEN MOVES.. HAVE TO STAY CALM..

GBTrudeau

GBTrudeau